United States Government Accountability Office

Report to the Chairman, Federal
Deposit Insurance Corporation

I0410978

July 2014

INFORMATION SECURITY

FDIC Made Progress in Securing Key Financial Systems, but Weaknesses Remain

GAO-14-674

GAO Highlights

Highlights of GAO-14-674, a report to the Chairman, Federal Deposit Insurance Corporation

INFORMATION SECURITY

FDIC Made Progress in Securing Key Financial Systems, but Weaknesses Remain

Why GAO Did This Study

The Federal Deposit Insurance Corporation (FDIC) has a demanding responsibility enforcing banking laws, regulating financial institutions, and protecting depositors. Because of the importance of FDIC's work, effective information security controls are essential to ensure that the corporation's systems and information are adequately protected from inadvertent or deliberate misuse, improper modification, unauthorized disclosure, or destruction.

As part of its audits of the 2013 financial statements of the Deposit Insurance Fund and the Federal Savings and Loan Insurance Corporation Resolution Fund administered by FDIC, GAO assessed the effectiveness of the corporation's controls in protecting the confidentiality, integrity, and availability of its financial systems and information. To do so, GAO examined security policies, procedures, reports, and other documents; tested controls over key financial applications; and interviewed FDIC personnel.

What GAO Recommends

GAO is recommending four actions for FDIC to enhance its information security management program. FDIC concurred with GAO's recommendations. In a separate report with limited distribution, GAO is recommending that FDIC take 21 specific actions to address weaknesses in security controls.

View GAO-14-674. For more information, contact Gregory C. Wilshusen at (202) 512-6244 or wilshuseng@gao.gov or Dr. Nabajyoti Barkakati at (202) 512-4499 or barkakatin@gao.gov.

What GAO Found

The Federal Deposit Insurance Corporation (FDIC) has implemented numerous information security controls intended to protect its key financial systems; nevertheless, weaknesses place the confidentiality, integrity, and availability of financial systems and information at unnecessary risk. During 2013, the corporation implemented 28 of the 39 open GAO recommendations pertaining to previously-reported security weaknesses that were unaddressed as of December 31, 2012. The table below details the status of previously-reported recommendations by year.

Status of Previously-Reported Information Security Recommendations

Year Reported	Not implemented at the beginning of 2013	Implemented during 2013	Not Implemented
2011	8[a]	7	1
2012	1[b]	0	1
2013	30	21	9
Total	39	28	11

Source: GAO analysis of FDIC data. | GAO-14-674

[a] FDIC had previously implemented 31 of the 38 recommendations GAO originally reported in 2011.
[b] FDIC had previously implemented 41 of the 42 recommendations GAO originally reported in 2012.

However, FDIC had not fully implemented controls for (1) identifying and authenticating the identity of users, (2) restricting access to sensitive systems and data, (3) encrypting sensitive data, (4) completing background reinvestigations for employees and (4) auditing and monitoring system access.

An underlying reason for many of these weaknesses is that FDIC did not fully or consistently implement aspects of its information security program. Specifically, FDIC did not:

- fully document and implement information security controls;
- ensure that employees and contractors received security awareness training;
- conduct ongoing assessments of security controls for all systems; and
- remediate agency identified weaknesses in a timely manner.

These weaknesses individually or collectively do not constitute either a material weakness or a significant deficiency for financial reporting purposes. Nevertheless, unless FDIC takes further steps to mitigate these weaknesses, the corporation's sensitive financial information and resources will remain exposed to unnecessary risk of inadvertent or deliberate misuse, improper modification, unauthorized disclosure, or destruction.

Contents

Abbreviations

CDR	Central Data Repository
CHRIS	Corporate Human Resources Information System
DCOM	Data Communications
FDIC	Federal Deposit Insurance Corporation
FFIEC	Federal Financial Institutions Examination Council
FIPS	Federal Information Processing Standard
FISMA	Federal Information Security Management Act
NIST	National Institute of Standards and Technology
POA&M	plan of action and milestones
SP	special publication
T&A	Time and Attendance
US-CERT	United States Computer Emergency Readiness Team

July 17, 2014

The Honorable Martin J. Gruenberg
Chairman
Federal Deposit Insurance Corporation

Dear Mr. Gruenberg:

The Federal Deposit Insurance Corporation (FDIC) has a demanding responsibility enforcing banking laws, regulating banking institutions, and protecting depositors. In carrying out its financial and mission-related operations, FDIC relies extensively on computerized systems. Because the corporation plays an important role in maintaining public confidence in the nation's financial system, issues that affect the confidentiality, integrity, and availability of the sensitive information maintained on its systems are of paramount concern. In particular, effective information security controls are essential to ensure that FDIC systems and information are being adequately protected from inadvertent or deliberate misuse, fraudulent use, improper disclosure, or destruction.

As part of our audit of FDIC's 2013 financial statements of the Deposit Insurance Fund and the Federal Savings and Loan Insurance Corporation Resolution Fund, we assessed the effectiveness of FDIC's information security controls over key financial systems, data, and networks. In our audit report, we concluded that FDIC maintained, in all material respects, effective internal control over financial reporting as of December 31, 2013, based on criteria established under *the Federal Managers' Financial Integrity Act of 1982*.[1]

In this report, we provide additional details on FDIC's information security controls over its computerized financial systems during 2013. Our objective was to determine the effectiveness of the corporation's controls in protecting the confidentiality, integrity, and availability of its financial systems and information. To do this, we examined FDIC information security policies, plans, and procedures; tested controls over its key financial applications; reviewed our prior reports to identify previously-reported weaknesses and assess the effectiveness of corrective actions

---

[1] 31 U.S.C. § 3512(c) and (d).

taken, and interviewed key agency officials. This work was performed to support our opinion on FDIC's internal control over financial reporting as of December 31, 2013.

We performed our work in accordance with U.S. generally accepted government auditing standards. We believe that our audit work provided a reasonable basis for our conclusion in this report. See appendix I for more details on our objective, scope, and methodology.

Background

Information security is a critical consideration for any agency that depends on information systems and computer networks to carry out its mission and is especially important for a government corporation such as FDIC, which has responsibilities to oversee the financial institutions that are entrusted with safeguarding the public's money. While the use of interconnected electronic information systems allows the corporation to accomplish its mission more quickly and effectively, this also exposes FDIC's information to threats from sources internal and external to the agency. Internal threats include errors, as well as fraudulent or malevolent acts by employees or contractors working within the agency. External threats include the ever-growing number of cyber-based attacks that can come from a variety of sources such as hackers, criminals, foreign nations, terrorists, and other adversarial groups.

Potential cyber attackers have a variety of techniques at their disposal, which can vastly enhance the reach and impact of their actions. For example, cyber attackers do not need to be physically close to their targets, their attacks can easily cross state and national borders, and they can preserve their anonymity. Additionally, advanced persistent threats— where an adversary that possesses sophisticated levels of expertise and significant resources can attack using physical and cyber methods to achieve its objectives[2]—pose increasing risks. Further, the interconnectivity among information systems presents increasing opportunities for such attacks. Indeed, reports of security incidents from

---

[2]These objectives typically include establishing/extending footholds within the IT infrastructure of the targeted agency for purposes of exfiltrating information; undermining or impeding critical aspects of a mission, program, or agency; or positioning itself to carry out these objectives in the future. An advanced persistent threat (1) pursues its objectives repeatedly over an extended period of time, (2) adapts to defenders' efforts to resist it, and (3) maintains the level of interaction needed to achieve its objectives.

federal agencies are on the rise. Specifically, the number of incidents reported by federal agencies to the United States Computer Emergency Readiness Team[3] (US-CERT) has increased dramatically in recent years: from 5,503 incidents reported in fiscal year 2006 to 60,753 incidents in fiscal year 2013.

Compounding the growing number and types of threats are the deficiencies in security controls on the information systems at federal agencies, which have resulted in vulnerabilities in both financial and nonfinancial systems and information. These deficiencies continue to place assets at risk of inadvertent or deliberate misuse, financial information at risk of unauthorized modification or destruction, and critical operations at risk of disruption. Accordingly, we have designated information security as a governmentwide high-risk area since 1997, a designation that remains in force today.[4]

Recognizing the highly networked nature of the federal computing environment, Congress enacted the *Federal Information Security Management Act* (FISMA) in December 2002.[5] One of the purposes of FISMA was to provide a comprehensive framework for ensuring the effectiveness of information security controls over information resources that support federal operations and assets. To accomplish this, FISMA requires each agency to develop, document, and implement an agencywide information security program to provide information security for the information and systems that support the operations and assets of the entity, using a risk-based approach to information security management. Such a program includes assessing risk; developing and implementing cost-effective security plans, policies, and procedures; providing specialized training; testing and evaluating the effectiveness of controls; planning, implementing, evaluating, and documenting remedial actions to address information security deficiencies; and ensuring continuity of operations.

---

[3]The Department of Homeland Security's federal information security incident center is hosted by US-CERT. When incidents occur, agencies are to notify the center.

[4]GAO, *High-Risk Series: Information Management and Technology*, GAO/HR 97 9 (Washington, D.C.: February 1997) and GAO-13-283 (Washington, D.C.: February 2013).

[5]FISMA was enacted as title III, *E-Government Act of 2002*, Pub. L. No. 107-347, 116 Stat. 2899, 2946 (Dec. 17, 2002).

FISMA also assigned to the National Institute of Standards and Technology (NIST) the responsibility for developing standards and guidelines that include minimum information security requirements. To this end, NIST has issued several special publications (SP) to provide guidance for agencies in implementing an information security program. For example, NIST SP 800-53 provides guidance to agencies on the selection and implementation of information security and privacy controls for systems and NIST Federal Information Processing Standards (FIPS) 199 provides requirements on how agencies should categorize their information system(s).

FDIC Is a Key Protector of Bank and Thrift Deposits

FDIC was created by Congress to maintain the stability of and public confidence in the nation's financial system by insuring deposits, examining and supervising financial institutions, and resolving troubled institutions. Congress created FDIC in 1933[6] in response to the thousands of bank failures that had occurred throughout the late 1920s and early 1930s.[7] FDIC identifies, monitors, and addresses risks to the Deposit Insurance Fund when a bank or thrift institution fails.

The Bank Insurance Fund and the Savings Association Insurance Fund were established as FDIC responsibilities under the *Financial Institutions Reform, Recovery, and Enforcement Act of 1989*, which sought to reform, recapitalize, and consolidate the federal deposit insurance system.[8] The act also designated FDIC as the administrator of the Federal Savings and Loan Insurance Corporation Resolution Fund, which was created to close out the business of the former Federal Savings and Loan Insurance Corporation and liquidate the assets and liabilities transferred from the former Resolution Trust Corporation.[9] The Bank Insurance Fund and the

---

[6]*Federal Deposit Insurance Corporation Act*, June 16, 1933, Ch. 89, § 8.

[7]FDIC is an independent agency of the federal government and receives no direct federal appropriations; it is funded by premiums that banks and thrift institutions pay for deposit insurance coverage and from earnings on investments in U.S. Treasury securities. Additionally, FDIC realizes some income from failed financial institutions for services it performs on their behalf.

[8]Pub. L. No. 101-73, § 211, 103 Stat. 183, 218-22 (Aug. 9, 1989).

[9]A third fund to be managed by FDIC, the Orderly Liquidation Fund, established by section 210 of the *Dodd-Frank Wall Street Reform and Consumer Protection Act*, Pub. L. No. 111-203, 124 Stat. 1376, 1506 (July 21, 2010), is unfunded and conducted no transactions during the fiscal years covered by this audit.

Savings Association Insurance Fund merged into the Deposit Insurance Fund on February 8, 2006, as a result of the passage of the Federal Deposit Insurance Reform Act of 2005.[10]

FDIC Relies on Computer Systems to Support its Mission and Financial Reporting

FDIC relies extensively on computerized systems to support its mission, including financial operations, and to store the sensitive information that it collects. The corporation uses local and wide area networks to interconnect its systems and a layered approach to security defense.

To support its financial management functions, FDIC uses a corporate-wide system that functions as a unified set of financial and payroll systems that are managed and operated in an integrated fashion; a system to calculate and collect FDIC deposit insurance premiums and Financing Corporation[11] bond principal and interest amounts from insured financial institutions; a Web-based application that provides full functionality to support franchise marketing, asset marketing, and asset management; an application and Web portal to provide acquiring institutions with a secure method for submitting required data files to FDIC; computer programs used to derive the corporation's estimate of losses from shared loss agreements; a system to request access to and receive permission for the computer applications and resources available to its employees, contractors, and other authorized personnel; and a primary receivership and subsidiary financial processing and reporting system.

Under FISMA, the Chairman of FDIC is responsible for, among other things, (1) providing information security protections commensurate with the risk and magnitude of the harm resulting from unauthorized access, use, disclosure, disruption, modification, or destruction of the agency's information systems and information; (2) ensuring that senior agency

---

[10]Pub. L. No. 109-171, Title II, Subtitle B, § 2102 (Feb. 8, 2006).

[11]The Financing Corporation, established by the *Competitive Equality Banking Act of 1987*, is a mixed-ownership government corporation with its primary purpose being to function as a financing vehicle for the Federal Savings and Loan Insurance Corporation. Effective December 12, 1991, as provided by the *Resolution Trust Corporation Refinancing, Restructuring and Improvement Act of 1991*, the Financing Corporation's ability to issue new debt was terminated. Outstanding Financing Corporation bonds, which are 30-year noncallable bonds with a principal amount of approximately $8.1 billion, mature in 2017 through 2019.

officials provide information security for the information and information systems that support the operations and assets under their control; and (3) delegating to the corporation's Chief Information Officer the authority to ensure compliance with the requirements imposed on the agency under FISMA.

The Chief Information Officer is responsible for developing and maintaining a corporatewide information security program and for developing and maintaining information security policies, procedures, and control techniques that address all applicable requirements. The Chief Information Officer also serves as the authorizing official with the authority to approve the operation of the information systems at an acceptable level of risk to the corporation.

The Chief Information Security Officer reports to the Chief Information Officer and serves as the Chief Information Officer's designated representative. The Chief Information Security Officer is responsible for (1) the overall support of assessment and authorization activities; (2) the development, coordination, and implementation of FDIC's security policy; and (3) the coordination of information security and privacy efforts across the corporation.

FDIC Has Made Progress in Securing Its Systems, but Improvements Are Still Needed

FDIC has designed and documented numerous information security controls intended to protect its key financial systems. However, many of these information security controls were not consistently implemented. An underlying reason for many of the information security weaknesses identified in our review is that FDIC had not always fully implemented key program activities. By mitigating known information security weaknesses and ensuring that access controls and other information security controls are consistently applied, FDIC could continue to reduce risks and better protect its sensitive financial information and resources from inadvertent or deliberate misuse, improper modification, unauthorized disclosure, or destruction.

FDIC Improved Access Controls, but Weaknesses Remain

A basic management objective for any agency is to protect the resources that support its critical operations and assets from unauthorized access. An agency can accomplish this by designing and implementing controls that are intended to prevent, limit, and detect unauthorized access to computer resources (e.g., data, programs, equipment, and facilities), thereby protecting them from unauthorized disclosure, modification, and loss. Specific access controls include identification and authentication of users, authorization restrictions, cryptography, audit and monitoring procedures, and incident response. Without adequate access controls, unauthorized users, including intruders and former employees, can surreptitiously read and copy sensitive data and make undetected changes or deletions for malicious purposes or for personal gain. In addition, authorized users could intentionally or unintentionally modify or delete data or execute changes that are outside of their authority.

Controls that ensure only authorized users have access to key systems have not always been completely implemented

While FDIC has made improvements in the access controls over its systems, weaknesses remain that may allow unauthorized users to access sensitive data or resources. For many computer systems, authorization and identification and authentication controls are a first line of defense in preventing unauthorized access to a system. NIST guidance[12] recommends that organizations implement controls to ensure that only authorized users can access the system. This includes, but is not limited to, uniquely identifying all users, requiring complex passwords, periodically reviewing access to the system, disabling accounts that no longer need access to the system, and assigning the lowest level of permission necessary for a task.

During 2013, FDIC improved controls for identifying and authenticating the identity of users by implementing 11 recommendations pertaining to access control weaknesses that we had previously identified and that were open as of December 31, 2012. For example, the corporation took steps to bolster identification and authentication controls or authorization controls, including the following:

- removing shared accounts from the PORTIA application;

- implementing complex passwords on the FireEye malware protection system; and

- reviewing and ensuring that users had appropriate rights to the Corporate Human Resources Information System (CHRIS) Time and Attendance (T&A) application, SharePoint sites, and UNIX system administration scripts.

Although improvements were made, FDIC did not always implement sufficient authorization controls on information systems that process the

---

[12]NIST, *Recommended Security Controls for Federal Information Systems and Organizations*, SP 800-53, revision 3 (Gaithersburg, Md.: August 2009).

corporation's financial statements and data. For example, periodic reviews were not always conducted on several systems to determine whether users who had access still needed to have that access to the system. Furthermore, user access requests were not always documented to ensure that users had received approvals for their access. We also noted weaknesses in automated and manual controls designed to disable user access after inactivity or a separation from the agency.

Although these weaknesses did not materially impact FDIC's financial statements, the systems are still vulnerable to unauthorized access and modification of data.

Implementation of Encryption Controls Improved, but Weaknesses Remain

Cryptography controls can be used to help protect the integrity and confidentiality of data and computer programs by rendering data unintelligible to unauthorized users and/or protecting the integrity of transmitted or stored data. Cryptography involves the use of mathematical functions called algorithms and strings of seemingly random bits called keys to, among other things, encrypt a message or file so that it is unintelligible to those who do not have the secret key needed to decrypt it, thus keeping the contents of the message or file confidential. NIST guidance states that the use of encryption by organizations can reduce the probability of unauthorized disclosure of information. NIST also recommends that organizations employ cryptographic mechanisms to prevent unauthorized disclosure of information during transmission, encrypt passwords while being stored and transmitted, and establish a trusted communications path between users and security functions of information systems.

FDIC improved its encryption controls by implementing the four recommendations pertaining to previously-identified control weaknesses. For example, FDIC improved cryptographic controls over Windows servers by implementing FIPS-compliant controls over remote administration and file transfer services. Additionally, FDIC implemented improved security over UNIX servers by encrypting passwords.

However, FDIC did not always ensure that sensitive financial information transmitted across its network was being adequately encrypted. These weaknesses, while not material in relation to FDIC's financial statements, nevertheless increase the risk that an individual could capture information such as user credentials or other sensitive data and use the information to gain unauthorized access to data and system resources.

| Auditing and monitoring of key financial systems continues to challenge FDIC | Audit and monitoring involves the regular collection, review, and analysis of auditable events for indications of inappropriate or unusual activity, and the appropriate investigation and reporting of such activity. Automated mechanisms may be used to integrate audit monitoring, analysis, and reporting into an overall process for investigation and response to suspicious activities. Audit and monitoring controls can help security professionals routinely assess computer security, perform investigations during and after an attack, and even recognize an ongoing attack. Audit and monitoring technologies include network and host-based intrusion detection systems, audit logging, security event correlation tools, and computer forensics. NIST SP 800-53 rev 3 states that organizations should review and analyze information system audit records for indications of inappropriate or unusual activity and report the findings to designated agency officials. Additionally, NIST states that information systems should produce audit records that sufficiently describe the nature of events. |

FDIC improved its audit and monitoring of controls by implementing two of the seven outstanding recommendations pertaining to previously-identified control weaknesses. Specifically, FDIC

- improved auditing of privileged Oracle accounts and users who connect to the database server with privileged roles for the Aggregate Asset Valuation Review (AAVR) system and

- implemented improved capability for maintaining an audit trail for Division of Insurance and Research Statistical Analysis System programs used to estimate the quarterly contingent loss reserve amounts for anticipated and unanticipated failures of insured institutions.

The five outstanding recommendations and the additional weaknesses found this year show that the audit and monitoring area warrants additional management attention. For example, FDIC did not always capture sufficient log data necessary for investigation of potential security incidents or log the actions of privileged database users. While these issues did not materially affect the corporation's financial statements, they nevertheless increase the risk that database systems could be compromised without detection and that the data input files used in deriving contingent loss reserve estimates for anticipated bank failures could lack integrity without reliance on extensive manual compensating controls that were effectively implemented.

Other Information System Controls Improved, but Weaknesses Need Mitigation

In addition to access controls, other important controls should be in place to ensure the confidentiality, integrity, and availability of an agency's information. These controls include policies, procedures, and techniques for managing the configuration of information systems, conducting background investigations for employees and contractors, and securely segregating incompatible duties. Although FDIC had implemented numerous controls in these areas, weaknesses continue to challenge the corporation in ensuring the confidentiality, integrity, and availability of its information and information systems.

FDIC did not adequately ensure that financial information systems were securely configured

Configuration management controls are intended to prevent unauthorized changes to information system resources (for example, software programs and hardware configurations) and to provide reasonable assurance that systems are configured and operating securely and as intended. NIST SP 800-53, revision 3 recommends, among other things, that agencies apply the most restrictive possible mode of security settings on IT products consistent with operational requirements and that they should identify, track, and deploy patches for systems and applications in their environment.

FDIC improved its configuration management controls by implementing three of four recommendations pertaining to previously-identified weaknesses. For example, FDIC had

- updated or eliminated the use of several products that were no longer supported by the vendor;

- enhanced the security of a database supporting the AAVR database; and

- applied critical patches to third party software on systems supporting financial processing.

However, FDIC was not consistently managing its configuration management process. For example, we identified additional critical patches that had not been applied to desktops and servers. Furthermore, FDIC has not developed secure baseline configurations that document minimum security settings and guide administrators in consistently securing corporation systems. These weaknesses place FDIC systems at risk of damage from accidental or intentional changes, which in turn, places the confidentiality, integrity, and availability of key financial data and systems at risk.

Background reinvestigations are not being performed in accordance with FDIC policy	FDIC had not performed background reinvestigations on employees who use and operate its financial applications. FDIC policy states that personnel in moderate- and low-risk positions should be subject to a background reinvestigation every 5 and 7 years, respectively. However, prior to fall 2013, FDIC did not perform these reinvestigations for personnel who had a security rating less than high risk. Without a background reinvestigation of personnel in moderate- and low-risk positions, FDIC decreases its chances of identifying personnel who may place its systems at risk and preventing internal fraudulent activity.
Incompatible roles and responsibilities are not documented for many key financial systems	To reduce the risk of error or fraud, duties and responsibilities for authorizing, processing, recording, and reviewing transactions should be separated to ensure that one user does not control all of the critical stages of a process. NIST SP 800-53, revision 3, states that, to prevent malevolent activity without collusion, organizations should separate the duties of users as necessary and implement separation of duties through assigned information system access authorization. In addition, FDIC policy on access control for IT resources states that, where required, access controls shall be used to enforce the principle of separation of duties to restrict the level of access and ability provided to any single user.

FDIC improved its controls for separating users' incompatible duties by implementing all three of the outstanding recommendations that were open as of December 31, 2012. Of note, it had identified and documented incompatible roles for the Resolution Data Aggregator application and created procedures to enforce those roles.

However, we identified additional areas this year where controls over separation of duties had not been fully implemented. Specifically, FDIC had not identified or document incompatible roles and responsibilities for several systems supporting financial processing. Furthermore, we identified an instance where developers could alter both development and production code, which could result in malicious code being introduced undetected by FDIC. |

FDIC Did Not Fully Implement Aspects of Its Information Security Management Program Thereby Limiting the Effectiveness of Information SecurityControls

An entitywide information security management program is the foundation of a security control structure and a reflection of senior management's commitment to addressing security risks. The security management program should establish a framework and continuous cycle of activity for assessing risk, developing and implementing effective security procedures, and monitoring the effectiveness of these procedures. Without a well-designed program, security controls may be inadequate; responsibilities may be unclear, misunderstood, or improperly implemented; and controls may be inconsistently applied. FISMA requires each agency to develop, document, and implement an information security program that, among other things, includes

- periodic assessments of the risk of unauthorized access, use, disclosure, disruption, modification, or destruction of information and information systems;

- policies and procedures that (1) are based on risk assessments, (2) cost effectively reduce information security risks to an acceptable level, (3) ensure that information security is addressed throughout the life cycle of each system, and (4) ensure compliance with applicable requirements;

- plans for providing adequate information security for networks, facilities, and systems;

- security awareness training to inform personnel of information security risks and of their responsibilities in complying with agency policies and procedures, as well as training personnel with significant security responsibilities for information security;

- periodic testing and evaluation of the effectiveness of information security policies, procedures, and practices, to be performed with a frequency depending on risk, but no less than annually, and that includes testing of management, operational, and technical controls for every system identified in the agency's required inventory of major information systems;

- a process for planning, implementing, evaluating, and documenting remedial actions to address any deficiencies in its information security policies, procedures, or practices; and

- procedures for detecting, reporting, and responding to security incidents.

FDIC had developed, documented, and implemented several elements of its corporate information security program, as illustrated by the following examples:

- FDIC is periodically assessing risks for its systems.

- The corporation has developed and documented security policies and procedures for securing its information systems and information.

- FDIC has established a general process to investigate network incidents.

Furthermore, FDIC had improved its implementation of information security controls over the financial systems and information included in our review by implementing many controls effectively and by implementing 28 of the 39 recommendations pertaining to unaddressed security weaknesses that were previously reported.

However, FDIC did not fully or consistently implement aspects of its information program. Specifically, FDIC did not:

- fully document and implement information security controls;

- ensure that employees and contractors received security awareness training;

- conduct ongoing assessments of security controls for all systems; and

- remediate agency identified weaknesses in a timely manner.

An underlying reason for many of the information security weaknesses identified in our review is that FDIC had not always fully implemented key program activities. Without addressing weaknesses in its information security program, FDIC may have limited ability to ensure that its security controls are adequately designed and operating effectively.

Security controls were not always documented in system security plans

Security controls for minor system security plans were not consistently and adequately documented at FDIC. NIST SP 800-53, revision 3 states that an information system security plan should describe the security controls in place or planned for meeting its security requirements. NIST SP 800-37, revision 1 adds that security control implementation should be documented in the security plan and include a functional description of the control implementation. However, system security plans at FDIC did not always identify security controls to be assessed, document the existence of contingency plans, or present risks identified through a risk assessment. Without documented security controls, the authorizing official may not have an accurate representation of the environment for approval, and weaknesses that are present in the environment may not be communicated. Table 1 identifies the criteria used to evaluate FDIC's security controls, the weakness identified, and FDIC's response to the identified weakness.

Table 1: Security Controls

Criteria	Weakness identified	FDIC response[a]
NIST SP 800-53, revision 3 states that an information system security plan should describe the security controls in place or planned for meeting its security requirements. NIST SP 800-37, revision 1 also states that security control implementation should be documented in the security plan and include a functional description of the control implementation.	**Security controls** Security controls in system security plans were not consistently and adequately documented. Specifically, the system security plan for some FDIC systems lacked these pertinent security controls information: • The CHRIS T&A system security plan lacked information such as the security controls to be assessed, the responsible parties and time frames for review and analysis of audit logs, and the process for testing software updates. • The system security plan for the PORTIA application did not address potential separation of duties issues, access controls over audit log data, or a process for assessing security risks. • The RIS system security plan did not include the results of a risk assessment, details for reviewing system enhancements, evidence of contingency plans, or a methodology for maintaining system documentation. Without documented security controls for all systems, the authorizing official may not have an accurate representation of the environment needing approval, and weaknesses that are present in the environment may not be communicated.	FDIC officials concurred and acknowledged that system security plans for minor applications, such as CHRIS T&A, PORTIA, and RIS are not as detailed as the system security plans for major applications. Further, officials stated that they will take steps to ensure that security control descriptions are adequate and that all required information is included.

Source: GAO analysis of FDIC data and Office of Inspector General reports, FISMA requirements, and NIST guidelines. | GAO-14-674

[a]We have not verified the effectiveness of any corrective actions that FDIC stated have been taken to address weaknesses.

Common security controls have not been documented and provided to authorizing officials

FDIC did not always document security controls for systems that we reviewed. NIST SP 800-53, revision 3 states that agencies should document common controls with sufficient detail to enable a security implementation that is compliant with organizational security program plan policies. Furthermore, NIST also states that control documentation should provide a functional description of the control implementation (including planned inputs, expected behavior, and expected outputs). However, FDIC did not document controls that it identified as common across the corporation and security controls for minor systems were not consistently and adequately documented. Without documenting common controls, the authorizing official may not have an accurate representation of the environment that is being approved, and weaknesses that are present in the environment may not be communicated. Additionally, changes in the common controls environment may not be communicated to the authorizing official prior to implementation in the environment. Table 2 identifies the criteria used to evaluate FDIC's common controls, the weakness identified, our recommendation, and FDIC's response to the identified weakness.

Table 2: Common Controls

Criteria	Weakness identified	FDIC response[a]
NIST SP 800-53, revision 3 states that an agency's information security program plan should provide sufficient information about the program management controls and common controls (including specification of parameters for any assignment and selection operations either explicitly or by reference) to enable an implementation that is unambiguously compliant with the plan and a determination of the risk to be incurred if the plan is implemented as intended.	**Common controls** Implementation descriptions for controls that FDIC identified as common across the corporation were not documented and provided to the authorizing official. Without documenting common controls, the authorizing official may not have an accurate representation of the environment that is up for approval, and weaknesses that are present in the environment may not be communicated. Additionally, changes in the common controls environment may not be communicated to the authorizing official prior to implementation in the environment.	FDIC officials concurred and stated that common control descriptions should be reviewed annually by the Designated Approving Authority (DAA). In addition, officials stated that information security and privacy staff would conduct an annual briefing to the DAA on the status of common controls, testing paradigm, issues for concern, and associated risk.

Source: GAO analysis of FDIC data and Office of Inspector General reports, FISMA requirements, and NIST guidelines. | GAO-14-674

[a]We have not verified the effectiveness of any corrective actions that FDIC stated have been taken to address weaknesses.

Security training has not been completed for all users with significant security responsibilities

Basic security awareness training and role-specific training for those who have been granted enhanced access is not being completed by all users at FDIC. FDIC policy states that organizations should ensure that all users take security awareness training on at least an annual basis. Additionally, FDIC policy states that all system administrators should take training that specifically outlines the rules of behavior for administrative access to the systems. However, 3 out of the 59 administrators who support selected systems had not completed the required role-based training for individuals with significant security responsibilities. As a result, users may not be aware of their security responsibilities and security concerns within the application, thus increasing risk to FDIC that users may unintentionally introduce vulnerabilities or disrupt system operations. Table 3 identifies the criteria used to evaluate FDIC's security training status, the weakness identified, and FDIC's response to the identified weakness.

Table 3: Security Training

Criteria	Weakness identified	FDIC response[a]
FDIC Policy 09-008 states that all general support system administrators must complete the "Rules of Behavior" training before they are granted any level of administrative access and must renew their training on an annual basis. FDIC Circular 1360.16 requires that new employees complete security awareness training upon receiving network access.	**Security training** Training had not been completed by all employees with system access and security responsibilities. Specifically, 3 out of the 59 administrators supporting in-scope platforms had not completed the administrator rules of behavior training during the year. Also, one user from a sample of 43 had not completed FDIC's basic security awareness training after being granted access to the FDIC network. Without appropriate security training, users may not be aware of their security responsibilities and security concerns within the system.	FDIC officials concurred and stated the following: • One administrator switched contracts and moved into the database administrator group, after which, the administrator completed the required training in January 2014. • Two administrators had not taken general support system rules of behavior training. FDIC stated that they will annually review compliance with the training requirement beginning November 20, 2014.

Source: GAO analysis of FDIC data and Office of Inspector General reports, FISMA requirements, and NIST guidelines. | GAO-14-674

[a]We have not verified the effectiveness of any corrective actions that FDIC stated have been taken to address weaknesses.

Control assessments were not performed as scheduled for all systems

FDIC had not performed a security control assessment for all its systems. NIST SP 800-53, revision 3 states that agencies should establish a continuous monitoring strategy that includes ongoing security controls assessments. Further, FDIC guidance requires that all its information systems undergo a scheduled independent security assessment. Although FDIC policies called for a control assessment during 2013 for one of its general support systems and a data repository, the corporation did not complete the assessment before the end of the year. Without performing a security controls assessment on a periodic basis, FDIC has limited assurance that the controls are operating effectively to protect its systems. Table 4 identifies the criteria used to evaluate FDIC's control assessment process, the weakness identified, and FDIC's responses to the identified weakness.

Table 4: Control Assessments

Criteria	Weakness identified	FDIC response[a]
NIST SP 800-53, revision 3 states that an agency should establish a continuous monitoring strategy and implement a continuous monitoring program that includes ongoing security control assessments in accordance with the organizational continuous monitoring strategy and that the assessment should include the technical, management, and operational security controls employed within and inherited by the information system.	**Control assessments** Controls were not monitored according to FDIC policy for two FDIC systems. Specifically, control assessments had not been performed in 2013 for the Data Communications (DCOM) and Federal Financial Institutions Examination Council (FFIEC) Central Data Repository (CDR) systems. FDIC did not complete the DCOM assessment before the end of the year. By not testing security controls on a periodic basis, FDIC cannot ensure that controls, especially those that are reliant on manual processes, are operating effectively.	FDIC officials concurred and stated that continuous controls testing has commenced on DCOM and that testing results are being or will be documented. In addition, a full security assessment of the FFIEC-CDR system was completed in November 2012 and a new FFIEC-CDR contract was signed in 2013. FFIEC worked with the contractor to finalize their continuous monitoring program after the contract award. The contractor began to conduct control assessments according to the methodology established, and the first report was issued in January 2014.

Source: GAO analysis of FDIC data and Office of Inspector General reports, FISMA requirements, and NIST guidelines. | GAO-14-674

[a]We have not verified the effectiveness of any corrective actions that FDIC stated have been taken to address weaknesses.

Identified security weaknesses are not being closed in a timely fashion

FDIC developed a Plan of Action and Milestones (POA&M) for identified security control weaknesses; however, the weaknesses were not being remediated in accordance with established deadlines. FDIC guidance requires that such a plan be developed and updated to track remedial actions. Of the 220 general and common control weaknesses recorded, 41 were open 1 to 75 days past their expected closure date, and 43 did not have an expected closure date. FDIC also tracked 134 application control weaknesses, of which 21 were open from 3 to 80 days beyond their expected closure date. FDIC stated that the targeted dates for remediating weaknesses are based on risk and resource availability, and, in some cases, higher-priority concerns could delay remedial actions.

Furthermore, the Inspector General reported deficiencies in the corporate information security program as well. For example, IT security awareness and specialized training for staff with security responsibilities were not fully addressed in the Division of Information Technology's IT security training plan. In addition, the FDIC Office of the Inspector General reported that a number of high- and moderate-risk open security vulnerabilities listed in FDIC's POA&M tracking system were open for more than two years. With security control weaknesses continuing beyond the accepted time frames, FDIC systems remain at risk of compromise. Table 5 identifies the criteria used to evaluate FDIC's POA&M process, weakness identified, and FDIC's response to the identified weakness.

Table 5: Plan of Action and Milestones

Criteria	Weakness identified	FDIC response[a]
FDIC Division of Information Technology Risk Management Program General Support System, Major Application System Security Plan Template, November 2013, requires that the POA&M be developed and updated for the information system to document planned remedial actions to correct weaknesses or deficiencies noted during the assessment of the security controls.	**Plan of action and milestones** Known weaknesses tracked in the POA&M were not being remediated in accordance with established deadlines. The FDIC Office of the Inspector General reported on this issue in its fiscal year 2013 FISMA report. Of the 220 general support system or common controls POA&M items, 41 were past their expected closure date, ranging from 1 to 75 days overdue, and 43 did not have an expected closure date listed. Of the 134 major/minor application POA&M items, 21 were past their expected closure date, ranging from 3 to 80 days overdue. By not adequately managing POA&M items to their accepted due dates, there may be weaknesses in the control environment that management is unknowingly or unwilling to accept for extended periods of time. **No recommendation will be made because the FDIC Office of Inspector General has previously made a recommendation in this area.**	FDIC agreed that POA&M management should improve so that leaders are aware of prioritized weaknesses for resource allocation decisions. FDIC officials stated that weaknesses were not remediated because, in some cases, higher-priority work delayed action. In others, the finding should have been closed, but actions were not taken to submit evidence for closure. POA&Ms are now being tracked using a management dashboard implemented in November 2013. Further, officials stated that a new metric was added to the Security and Privacy dashboard to highlight findings that have been open for a prolonged period and closer management attention to these data should address the weakness identified.

Source: GAO analysis of FDIC data and Office of Inspector General reports, FISMA requirements, and NIST guidelines. | GAO-14-674

[a]We have not verified the effectiveness of any corrective actions that FDIC stated have been taken to address weaknesses.

Conclusions

FDIC has made progress toward strengthening many information security controls over its financial systems and information, but weaknesses remain. Specifically, FDIC has taken steps to improve access controls to ensure only valid, authorized, and approved users have access to its systems. Further, the corporation had developed, documented, and implemented many elements of its corporate information security program.

However, there are still areas of weakness in controlling access to key financial systems and in continuing to implement a comprehensive security management program. An underlying reason for many of the information security weaknesses identified in our review is that FDIC had not always fully implemented key program activities.

Given that federal agencies face an evolving array of cyber-based threats to information and information systems and that attackers have a variety of increasingly sophisticated attack techniques at their disposal, it is vitally important that FDIC address the remaining weaknesses in information security controls—both old and new—as part of its ongoing efforts to mitigate the risks from cyber attacks and to ensure the confidentiality, integrity, and availability of its financial and sensitive information. Although we do not consider these weaknesses individually or collectively to be either a material weakness or a significant deficiency for financial reporting purposes, unless FDIC takes further steps to mitigate these weaknesses, the corporation's sensitive financial information and resources will remain exposed to unnecessary risk of inadvertent or deliberate misuse, improper modification, unauthorized disclosure, or destruction.

Recommendations for Executive Action

To help strengthen access controls and other information security controls over key financial information, systems, and networks, we recommend that the Chairman of FDIC direct the Chief Information Officer to take the following four actions:

1. Document security controls descriptions for all systems to describe the control thoroughly and ensure that all the required information is included.

2. Document and maintain a description for each common control in an appropriate document, such as system security plans or other authoritative documents.

3. FDIC should ensure that those with administrative-level access have completed the requisite "Rules of Behavior" training upon receiving access and each year after that.

4. Perform control assessments for FFIEC CDR and DCOM in accordance with the frequency established.

In a separate report with limited distribution, we are also making 21 detailed recommendations consisting of actions to be taken to correct specific information security weaknesses related to access control, encryption, audit and monitoring, configuration management, segregation of duties, and background reinvestigations.

GAO-14-674 FDIC 2013 Information Security

Agency Comments and our Evaluation

In providing written comments (reprinted in app. II) on a draft of this report, the Deputy to the Chairman and Chief Financial Officer of FDIC stated that all corrective actions for the four new recommendations have been or will be completed by December 31, 2014. FDIC officials also provided an attachment detailing their concurrence with our four recommendations, and included language clarifying their responses to our recommendations, which we have incorporated into the report as appropriate.

We are also sending copies of this report to interested congressional parties.

If you have any questions regarding this report, please contact Gregory C. Wilshusen at (202) 512-6244 or Dr. Nabajyoti Barkakati at (202) 512-4499. We can also be reached by e-mail at wilshuseng@gao.gov and barkakatin@gao.gov. Key contributors to this report are listed in appendix III.

Gregory C. Wilshusen
Director, Information Security Issues

Dr. Nabajyoti Barkakati
Director, Center for Science, Technology, and Engineering

Appendix I: Objective, Scope, and Methodology

The objective of this information security review conducted as part of our audit of the Federal Deposit Insurance Corporation's (FDIC) financial statements of the Deposit Insurance Fund and the Federal Savings and Loan Insurance Corporation Resolution Fund was to determine the effectiveness of FDIC's controls in protecting the confidentiality, integrity, and availability of the corporation's financial systems and information.

The scope of our audit included an examination of FDIC information security policies, plans, and practices; controls over key financial applications; and interviews with key agency officials in order to (1) assess the effectiveness of corrective actions taken by FDIC to address weaknesses we previously reported and (2) determine whether any additional weaknesses existed. This work was performed in support of our opinion on internal control over financial reporting as it relates to our audits of the calendar year 2013 and 2012 financial statements of the two funds administered by FDIC.

To determine whether controls over key financial systems and information were effective, we considered the results FDIC's actions to mitigate previously-reported weaknesses that remained open as of December 31, 2012, and performed audit work at FDIC facilities in Arlington, Virginia. We concentrated our evaluation primarily on the controls for applications and enterprise database applications associated with financial processing, such as the New Financial Environment; Communication, Capability, Challenge, and Control System; PORTIA; Identity Access Management System; programs, data, and systems supporting the preparation of the estimates of losses and costs due to shared loss agreements; and general support systems. Our selection of the systems to evaluate was based on consideration of systems that directly or indirectly support the processing of material transactions that are reflected in the funds' financial statements.

Our audit methodology was based on the *Federal Information System Controls Audit Manual*,[1] which contains guidance for reviewing information system controls that affect the confidentiality, integrity, and availability of computerized information.

---

[1]GAO, *Federal Information System Controls Audit Manual* (FISCAM), GAO-09-232G (Washington, D.C.: Feb. 2009).

Using standards and guidance from the National Institute of Standards
and Technology, FDIC, and other third parties, as well as FDIC's policies,
procedures, and practices, we evaluated controls by:

- observing methods for providing secure data transmissions across the
  network to determine whether sensitive data were being encrypted;

- analyzing user and application system authorizations to determine
  whether they had more permissions than necessary to perform their
  assigned functions;

- assessing configuration settings to evaluate settings used to audit
  security-relevant events;

- evaluating the control configurations of selected servers and database
  management systems;

- analyzing configuration changes made to applications and programs
  to determine whether they were being controlled, documented,
  authorized, validated, reviewed, and tested;

- inspecting key servers and workstations to determine whether critical
  patches had been installed and were up to date; and

- examining access responsibilities to determine whether incompatible
  functions were segregated among different individuals.

Using the requirements of the Federal Information Security Management
Act, which establishes elements for an agencywide information security
program, we evaluated FDIC's implementation of its security program by:

- analyzing security plans for key financial systems to determine
  whether management, operational, and technical controls had been
  documented and whether security plans had been updated regularly
  in accordance with NIST requirements;

- reviewing training records for administrators to determine if they had
  received necessary training identified in FDIC policy;

- reviewing ongoing assessments of security controls to determine if
  they had been completed as scheduled; and

- analyzing plans of actions and milestones to determine if weaknesses
  were being tracked, managed and remediated.

We also discussed with key security representatives and management
officials whether information security controls were in place, adequately
designed, and operating effectively.

To determine the status of FDIC's actions to correct or mitigate previously-reported information security weaknesses, we identified and reviewed its information security policies, procedures, and guidance. We reviewed prior GAO reports to identify previously-reported weaknesses and examined FDIC's corrective action plans to determine which weaknesses FDIC had reported as being corrected. For those instances where FDIC reported it had completed corrective actions, we assessed the effectiveness of those actions.

We performed our work in accordance with U.S. generally accepted accounting standards. We believe that our audit work provided a reasonable basis for our conclusion in this report.

Appendix II: Comments from the Federal Deposit Insurance Corporation

Federal Deposit Insurance Corporation
550 17th Street NW, Washington, D.C. 20429-9990   Deputy to the Chairman and CFO

July 9, 2014

Mr. Gregory C. Wilshusen
Director, Information Security Issues
Dr. Nabajyoti Barkakati
Director, Center for Technology and Engineering
U.S. Government Accountability Office
Washington, D.C. 20548

Dear Mr. Wilshusen and Dr. Barkakati:

Thank you for the opportunity to comment on the U.S. Government Accountability Office's (GAO) draft audit report titled, Information Security: FDIC Made Progress in Securing Key Financial Systems but Weaknesses Remain; GAO-14-674.

The GAO's report contains four recommendations to assist FDIC in further strengthening its information security controls. The expected completion dates of actions to address the recommendations are included in Attachment 1. All corrective actions will be completed by December 31, 2014 or have already been completed.

Once again, we thank you for your past contributions and your work on this year's audit. We look forward to continuing our positive working relationship during the 2014 audit and beyond. If you have any questions relating to the FDIC management response, please contact James H. Angel, Jr., Deputy Director, Corporate Management Control Branch, Division of Finance, at 703-562-6456.

Sincerely,

Steven O. App
Deputy to the Chairman and
Chief Financial Officer

Attachments
cc: James H. Angel, Jr.,
        Bret Edwards
        Diane Ellis
        Martin Henning
        Craig Jarvill
        Arleas Upton Kea
        Audit Committee

Appendix III: GAO Contacts and Staff Acknowledgements

GAO Contacts	Gregory C. Wilshusen, (202) 512-6244, wilshuseng@gao.gov Dr. Nabajyoti Barkakati, (202) 512-4499, barkakatin@gao.gov
Staff Acknowledgments	In addition to the individuals named above, Gary Austin, Nick Marinos, and Christopher Warweg, (assistant directors), William Cook, Nancy Glover, Kenneth Johnson, Thomas Johnson, Krzysztof Pasternak, and Daniel Swartz made key contributions to this report.